I Hear the Prophet Callin'

Christmas Story from Prophecy to Fulfillment

Music and Lyrics by

Pepper Choplin

Editor: Larry Pugh

Music Engraving: Jeanette Dotson

Cover Design: Nancy Chifala

Jeff Richards

ISBN: 978-1-4291-0760-0

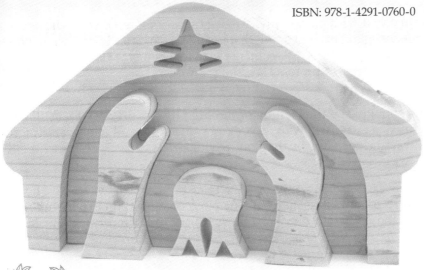

Foreword

People remember fondly a hometown World Series team from twenty years ago. However, they are *ecstatic* about a newly won championship. In the same manner, we have all sung, read, and dramatized the Christmas story year after year. However, we need to approach it as if it is brand new. We need to celebrate as if the events have just occurred.

It is not our place to make something new of the Christmas story, but it is our place to tell the true story in a fresh way so the listener will hear it as if for the first time. It is my desire to offer to you a fresh way to experience and sing of Christ's birth.

As I have called upon folk styles to celebrate the story, you will hear those distinct musical flavors: Appalachian, Irish, Latin, Cajun, and Early American. Something stirs within my soul as I hear their timeless rhythms, harmonies, and melodies. It seems a natural fit to pair this authentic and sometimes earthy music with the true story of the Gospel.

There are optional scripture readings noted in several of the pieces. Rather than the traditional narration, however, I've used a recurring melodic theme to lead the way through the events. The musical narration directs us to the different "stations" of the Christmas story:

I hear…

> *the prophet calling…*
>
> *a mother singing…*
>
> *the shepherds calling…*

I see the star of glory…

I hear the people singing…

This musical works very well with piano only. To give the work a fresh voice, however, Stan Pethel has provided a lighter orchestration that includes strings and percussion with a few wind instruments. Other optional instruments such as a penny whistle, hammered dulcimer, and accordion bring an extra folk flavor to the work.

The choir and soloists should keep the "telling of the story" as its primary focus. Paint the scenes musically, preach the gospel with fervor and conviction, and rejoice at the gift of what Christmas always brings—the birth of our Savior, Jesus Christ.

My prayer is that this music will serve you as you celebrate the story anew. May we bond together—composer, director, and musicians—to help our congregation experience this wonderful story. May God bless in a new way as we all try to be faithful to our most blessed tasks.

May God bless you in your ministry of music,

—*Pepper Choplin*

Contents

Companion Products

65/2005L	SATB Score
30/2494L	Instrumental Ensemble Score and Parts by Stan Pethel *Pennywhistle (or Fl), Fl, Alto Flute, Recorder (or Fl), Ob/Eng Hn, Hn, Autoharp (opt.),* *Hammered Dulcimer, Accordion (opt.), Mandolin, Guitar, 3 Perc, Vln 1 & 2,* *Vla, Cello, Bass*
99/2528L	Performance CD (includes SATB and SAB versions)
99/2529L	Bulk Performance CDs (10 pak)
99/2530L	Accompaniment CD
99/2531L	SA/TB Part-dominant Rehearsal CDs (reproducible)
99/2532L	SA/B Part-dominant Rehearsal CDs (reproducible)
65/2007L	Performance CD/SATB Score Combination
65/2008L	Performance CD/SAB Score Combination

Listen to the Story

Words and Music by
Pepper Choplin

6

Lis-ten,—— God is com-ing,—— God is com-ing—— to the earth.

Lis-ten,—— hear the sto-ry—— told so man-y—— times be-fore.

Lis-ten,—— hear the sto-ry—— told so man-y times be-fore.

*Cued notes are optional additional notes throughout.

un - to us a Child is born to all. His

all.

gov - ern - ment shall be up - on His shoul-ders, He is called Em - man - u -

el. Come and lis - ten to God's ho - ly

Lis - ten, come and lis - ten_____ to the sto - ry_____

Lis - ten_____ to the sto - ry_____ like you've

Lis - ten_____ to the sto - ry_____ like you've

_____ like you've nev - er_____ heard be - fore.

nev - er_____ heard be - fore.

nev - er_____ heard be - fore.

Lis-ten— to the sto-ry— of the com-ing— of the

Lord. Joy to the world, joy to the world. Get

Joy to the world. Get

cresc.
read-y, the Lord will come!——— *ff*

cresc.
read-y, the Lord will come!——— *ff*

cresc. *ff*

I Hear the Prophet Callin'

SAB and Solo

Based on
Isaiah 35:1-2, 4-6, and 40:3

Words and Music by
Pepper Choplin

Optional narration #1: Isaiah 40:3-5

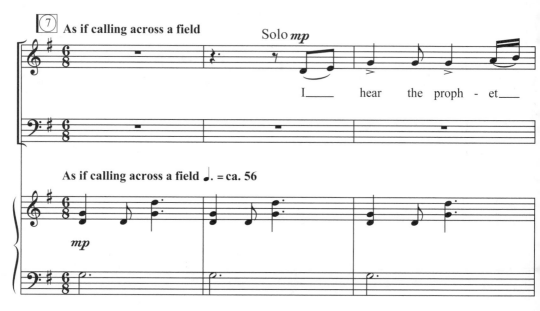

ML

hear the proph - et___ call - in', "Pre - pare the way___ of the___

Lord." Come and make___ straight the way in the des - ert, a

high - way___ for_____ our___ God. Come and make___ straight the way in the

des - ert, pre - pare the way__ of the__ Lord. Pre -

pare the way__ of the__ Lord. I__

hear I - sa - iah call - in', "Fear__ not, your God____ will__

call - in', "Pre - pare the way__ of the__ Lord." I___

hear the proph - et call - in', "Pre - pare the way__ of the__

Lord, pre - pare ye the way of the__ Lord."_____

The People Who Walk in Darkness

Isaiah 9:2 and **Isaiah 40:5**

Words and Music by
Pepper Choplin

Optional narration #2: Isaiah 9:2 (under the introduction)

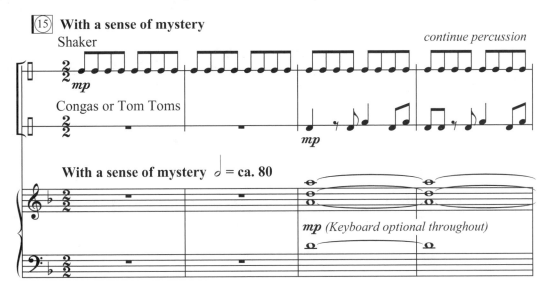

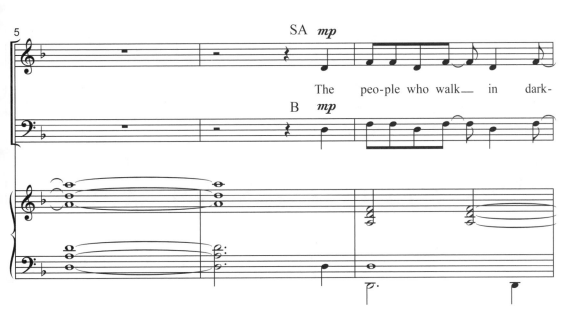

24

- ness have seen a great light. The

peo-ple who walk__ in dark - ness have seen a great

light. Now, lift up your eyes, see the

glo - ry of ____ the Lord. Now, lift up your

eyes, see the glo - ry of ____ the Lord, _____ and

all flesh will see it to - geth - er. _____ The

The

eyes, see the glo - ry of___ the Lord. Now,

lift up your eyes, see the glo - ry of___ the Lord,___ and

all flesh will see it to - geth - er,_____ and

all flesh will see it to - geth - er.

A - rise and shine, your light has

come to the peo - ple who walk in dark - ness!

I Hear a Mother Singin'

Female Solo

Words and Music by
Pepper Choplin

Optional narration #3: Luke 2:1, 3-7

ten - der lul - la - by._____ I_____

hear a moth - er___ sing - in'._____

segue

pp *rit.*

Rockin' Slow and Even

Tune inspired by
How Can I Keep from Singing?
by Ira D. Sankey

Words and Music by
Pepper Choplin

Now Mar-y holds her tin-y child, her prec-ious gift from hea-ven. His cra-dle is— her— lov-ing arms, she's

36

65/2006L-36

38

There in the Same Country

Based on
Luke 2:8-20

Words and Music by
Pepper Choplin

Optional narration #4: Luke 2:8-12 (Start music at verse 11. "Today in the town...")

Christ_____ the Lord, He is Christ,_____ the Lord, He is

Christ, Christ,_____ the Lord, Christ,_____ the

Christ,_____ the ho - ly Lord."

Lord, ho - ly Lord."

This shall be to you a sign: wrapped in swad-dling clothes you'll find

from the ho - ly host would rise a joy - ous pro - cla -

ma - tion. And they said, "Glo - ry to— God." They said,

"Glo - ry, glo - ry to

"Glo - ry to— God." They said, "Glo - ry to— God on

God, all glo - ry to God, to our God on

come, let us a-dore Him. O come, let us a-dore Him,

Christ, the Lord. There, in the same coun-try,

shep-herds bowed to wor - ship the new-born King.

I Hear the Shepherds Callin'

Female Solo

Words and Music by
Pepper Choplin

www.lorenz.com

JD

Go Tell It

Words by
John W. Work, Jr.

Music by **Pepper Choplin**
Tune: GO TELL IT
an African American spiritual

*Optional narration #5: Luke 2:17-18, 20
(before the music begins).*

JD

ev - 'ry - where. Go, tell it on the moun - tain that

Je - sus Christ — is born." Down in a low - ly

man - ger, the hum - ble Christ was born, and

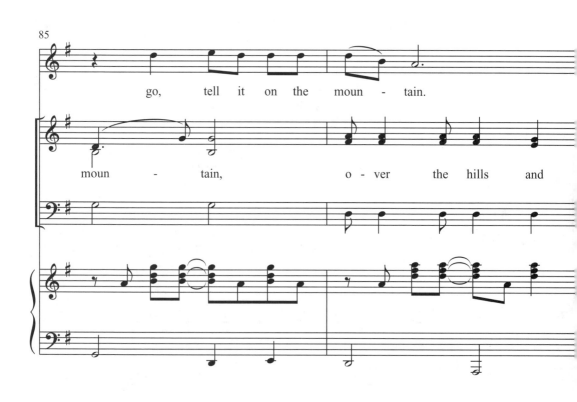

I See the Star of Glory

Female Solo or Duet

Words and Music by
Pepper Choplin

Lyrics:
I____ see the star of glo - ry a - ris - in' in____ the____ east.____ I____ see the star of

glo - ry   a - ris - in'— in— the— east.   And— I—

know   the star— will lead— me   un - to   the Prince— of

Peace.   I— see   the star   of— glo - ry   a -

ris - in'— in— the— east.

A Star Rising in the East

Optional narration #6: Matthew 2:1, 9-11, alt (before music begins)

Words and Music by
Pepper Choplin

star,_____ shin-ing o'er the earth,_____ the

her - ald of_____ a roy - al birth._____

SA **mf**
U - pon the dark - ness shines a light,

B **mf**

mf

and from the Lord,_____ there comes a sign._____

Be - hold, a vir - gin shall con - ceive

rit. e dim.

and bear a son,_____ "Em -

rit. e dim.

and shall call His name, "Em -

rit. e dim.

star,_____ a wit-ness of His care,_____

_____ the____ an - swer_____ to the

cresc.

an - cient prayer._____ For un - to

mf *f*

Won - der-ful Coun - sel - or, Al - might - y

God, _____ the Ev - er - last - ing

God, the Ev - er - last - ing Fa - ther, the

poco a poco dim.

Fa - ther, the Ev - er - last - ing Fa - ther, the

poco a poco dim.

Ev - er - last - ing Fa - ther, the Ev - er - last - ing

poco a poco dim.

Ev - er - last - ing Fa - ther, the Prince of

Fa - ther,

Peace.

A

star_____ shin-ing through the night,_____ il -

lu - min-ing_____ the Way,_____ the_____

Truth, the Life._____

I Hear the People Singin'

Words and Music by
Pepper Choplin

come." We shall re - joice with joy__ and sing - ing and

see the__ glo - ry of__ God. We shall re - joice__ with joy__ and

sing - ing and see the glo - ry of__ God, and

Music: ANTIOCH by George F. Handel, 1742; Text: Isaac Watts, 1719

Lord is come: Let earth re-ceive her King. Let ev - 'ry— heart— and heav'n and na-ture— sing, and— pre-pare— Him— room— and heav'n and na-ture— sing, and— heav'n and na-ture— sing and— heav'n, and heav'n— and na - ture

sing. No more let sins and

sor - rows grow, nor thorns in - fest the

ground. He comes— to— make— His bless - ings— flow— far

far

ground; He comes to make His bless-ings flow

far as the curse is found, far as the curse is found,

He comes to make His bless-ings flow.

82

Optional Narration
Taken from NIV, alt.

Listen to the Story (page 5)

Narration 1: *Isaiah 40:3-5*

A voice of one calling: "In the desert prepare the way for the Lord; make straight in the wilderness a highway for our God.

Every valley shall be raised up, every mountain and hill made low; the rough ground shall become level, the rugged places a plain.

And the glory of the Lord will be revealed, and all mankind together will see it. For the mouth of the Lord has spoken."

I Hear the Prophet Callin' (page 14)

Narration 2: *Isaiah 9:2*

The people walking in darkness have seen a great light; on those living in the land of the shadow of death, a light has dawned.

The People Who Walk in Darkness (page 23)

Narration 3: *Luke 2:1, 3-7*

In those days Caesar Augustus issued a decree that a census should be taken of the entire Roman world. And everyone went to his own town to register.

So Joseph also went up from the town of Nazareth in Galilee to Judea, to Bethlehem, the town of David, because he belonged to the house and line of David. He went there to register with Mary, who was pledged to be married to him and was expecting a child. While they were there, the time came for the baby to be born, and she gave birth to her firstborn, a son. She wrapped him in cloths and placed him in a manger, because there was no room for them in the inn.

I Hear a Mother Singin' (page 33)

Rockin' Slow and Even (page 35)

Narration 4: *Luke 2:8-12*

And there were shepherds living out in the fields nearby, keeping watch over their flocks at night. An angel of the Lord appeared to them, and the glory of the Lord shone around them, and they were terrified. But the angel said to them, "Do not be afraid. I bring you good news of great joy that will be for all the people. Today in the town of David, a Savior has been born to you; He is Christ the Lord. This will be a sign to you: You will find a baby wrapped in cloths and lying in a manger."

There in the Same Country (page 42)

I Hear the Shepherds Callin' (page 50)

Narration 5: *Luke 2:17-18, 20*

When they had seen Him, they spread the word concerning what had been told them about this Child, and all who heard it were amazed at what the shepherds said to them. The shepherds returned, glorifying and praising God for all the things they had heard and seen, which were just as they had been told.

Go Tell It (page 51)

I See the Star of Glory (page 63)

Narration 6: *Matthew 2:1, 9-11*

After Jesus was born in Bethlehem in Judea, during the time of King Herod, Magi from the east came to Jerusalem. They had seen a star in the east and had come to worship Him. The star went ahead of them until it stopped over the place where the Child was. When they saw the star, they were overjoyed. On coming to the house, they saw the Child with His mother, Mary, and they bowed down and worshiped Him. Then they opened their treasures and presented Him with gifts of gold and of incense and of myrrh.

A Star Rising in the East (page 65)

I Hear the People Singin' (page 74)

Performance Notes

I am always delighted to hear how people have applied their creativity to the presentation of my music. There are many possibilities to enhance this work. Many of you will use full drama; others will use visuals on your projection systems. I have had much positive response to projecting the text of our music on the screen. Though we strive toward clear articulation, people say that they like to reflect on the words and let them "sink in" as they listen.

Generally, I think much of the music works best with a brighter, vibrant tone and consonants. I have written in many indications for choir member to slide and scoop just a bit to enhance the styles used. Here are some specific notes about each piece.

Listen to the Story **(page 5)**

There should be an electric sense of anticipation throughout—a feeling of leaning forward as we prepare to hear the story.

I Hear the Prophet Callin' **(page 14)**

The tone should be sturdy and solid with plenty of emphasis on the downbeat. Notice the call for stomps beginning in m. 20. I have found it effective for just a few choir members to stomp strongly on each beat 1 and more softly on beat 2, ending on beat 1 of m. 68. Sing with no vibrato to achieve a more primitive sound. The spirit and the singing should come from deep down in the soul.

The People Who Walk in Darkness **(page 23)**

Mystery and revelation are key words for this piece. The beginning should have more consonants than tone as the choir sings with wide-eyed expectancy. Be ready to exploit the dramatic possibilities in m. 46 as it builds to a vibrant climax in m. 63.

I Hear a Mother Singin' **(page 33)**

The soloist should reach down and find the warmth and richness of a mother's tone to lead the listener into the next phase of the story.

Rockin' Slow and Even **(page 35)**

A gentle emphasis and expansion on beat 1 of each measure will propel the song and accentuate the melody's beauty and shape. In mm 36-48, enjoy the rise and fall of the musical breath, especially as the men and women rise at different points in mm 45-48.

There in the Same Country (page 42)

A little accent on each downbeat will give this piece a hearty folk sound. This is basically the scripture put to music. As you sing, "preach" the words a bit. Whenever a section has sixteenth notes, they should "lean" into the music. At m. 40, when the mood turns to quiet worship, sing with intimacy, but don't go too slowly. Measure 55 is meant to be a reflection on the beginning of the song.

Go Tell It (page 51)

I've always felt a little more license to enjoy the story of the shepherds. A Cajun-style arrangement of the spiritual seems to match their earthiness. Have fun as you begin at m. 5 with a hushed intensity, growing to an exuberant celebration in m. 16. Notice the accents throughout and punch those places. Be ready to party at m. 72. Really "preach" at m. 81 with the soloist leading the way at m. 84.

See the Star of Glory (page 63)

A rather straight tone will serve the style here, especially if sung as a duet. Make sure each sixteenth note has good energy. Remember to use plenty of emphasis on each downbeat.

A Star Rising in the East (page 65)

A good, smooth feeling on a foundation of a strong feel of 2 will help this piece live. There are several dramatic moments; look for these in mm 36-40, 57-59, 68-76, and m. 98 to the end.

Hear the People Singin' (page 74)

After the prologue, m. 36 is the time to release the joy of the event. Let the rhythm of the text dance and sparkle. I always like to have the choir explode the "j" a bit each time they say "joy." This is especially needed at m. 86 as it drives to the end.